101 Quotes That Will Change Your Life

101 QUOTES THAT WILL CHANGE YOUR LIFE

101 Quotes: Volume I

Topher Pike

Written for anyone with a dream hidden for too long

Hit me up on Instagram
www.instagram.com/topherpikebooks

Exclusive Giveaways and Free Signed Books

Become an Insider and Get Full Access

FREE BOOK
TOPHERPIKE.COM/FREE-BOOK
A Spiritual Journey of Self Discovery
BLACK BIRD
TOPHER PIKE
A Spiritual Journey of Self Discovery
BLACK BIRD
TOPHER PIKE

CONTENTS

"The way to get rid of darkness is with light." – *Joseph Murphy*

Preface

You do not know my name because my story has yet to be written. As an unknown but inspired writer, I am going to say little about my previous story in this book because this is my first chapter. I will not write the story of my past because the belief I have in my future is so clear that I can only see what is possible and already here. I have learned things about myself since I have chosen to open my eyes to a new way of thinking, and I'm stronger today than I was yesterday.

After intense soul-searching, I now have a different perspective on life and have finally found a purpose. I am grateful for my life today, but I am also grateful for the life I can see tomorrow.

I am only writing this book because I can finally hear the voice that I have been afraid to free. I believe this voice needs to be heard by anyone with a dream for something unbelievable.

If you have a dream that you have been afraid to unleash, I'm here to tell you it's possible. It's possible to get anything you want in life, and this book will be my example—an example for those who decide their fears are not real and reality is the fantasy they choose to believe. A place where fears are only a part of yesterday's circumstances.

I now live in a world where the image I see brings me the excitement I need to fulfill my dreams of a better life for my family.

This book is the first chapter in a life I always imagined was possible. This book will astonish any reader who believes his or her life has already been written. Today, I can hear my future knocking because I finally dare to open the door.

I have found a key to unlock my deepest dreams and desires, and I'm here to tell you that it's not the only copy. Tomorrow, I will be a best-selling author with a clearer vision for my next chapter.

If you believe in a higher power than yourself, you are on the right frequency. If you don't believe your perfect life is possible, you need to read this book.

It will not be a comfortable journey toward the life you always imagined was possible. Every day will be a fight to let go of your doubts and truly capture your vision of perfection. You may only see it in your mind, but make sure you see it every day. See it as if you cannot see any other possible outcome. I hope this book will give you the strength to rise above normality and create a path that only you can see.

Nobody else can change the way you think or the way you live, but your mind and body together can change the way you see the world. I hope you can feel the power in my words and use your thoughts to inspire a new way of thinking. My story starts today, and I'm inviting you to become a character in the first chapter of my journey. Join me and experience the power and joy of freeing your mind and releasing your dreams.

I understand that the power I have been given is the greatest gift I will ever receive, and I believe I must give something back. This book is my first mass production. I think that life can be everything you imagine if you believe in yourself and believe in the goals and vision you have put forth. I see the strength in the belief in my dreams and finally understand how to embrace their power and reality.

The choice is yours in how you embrace the words I have written in this book. I believe you have the power to create your future, but only you can believe it's possible. Use my words to inspire your belief that you can capture the key to a door only you can open.

I will become a successful author, and once this happens, you will have no choice but to believe in my way of thinking. What dream are you afraid to unlock? If you believe in my words, share my book with anyone who has forgotten to fight for their dreams.

Fantasy will soon become a reality when you believe your dreams are real. The words you read in this book have given me the strength to see a world that already exists. It exists not only in my mind but in every step I take toward positivity.

Acknowledgement

I wouldn't have written this book without love and support from my better half. My wife has not only been by my side for every transformational moment in my new life, but she has also been fighting for her beliefs in the impossible. She has courageously joined my journey despite a lack of confidence in the beauty that she possesses.

Her fight has made my journey even more pronounced because I can see the life she deserves, even when she thinks she is fighting a losing battle. I am here to tell her that I'm in her corner, and the twelfth round is a knockout. We will have everything we want in life because life is beautiful. Life is not about being the manager of awesome but being awesome when life hits you hard. She gets that. Hitting back is not about fighting your anger but understanding that your strength lies in a ring that was never built. She is not only an amazing mother but a person who can shine in the face of defeat and stare down her deepest fear.

The reality is that life is about to become the dream we have found together. I hope she never underestimates the love I have for her and always appreciates and is grateful for the love she finds within. She is beautiful just the way she is.

No words can describe my love for a woman who is afraid to love herself. Her support cannot be measured, but I hope my words can inspire her always to build a ring worth her beauty.

Dedication

This book is dedicated to a woman I have never met but a voice I hear every day. A voice that I have listened to many times before. It wasn't until I decided to go after everything I wanted in life and change my way of thinking that I could finally hear the power of her words. My daughter would play her song on repeat until our grease-filled tablet would die from exhaustion.

I would hear her song aggressively playing in my head every day I forced myself to get out of bed and join the herd. I ran through my daily tasks with uncontrollable fear and disappointment in the life I created. After seven long days of self-reflection, I can now see clearly. I decided to change the way I see my future and how I use my thoughts.

It was only after this transformation of mind, body, and soul that I could finally understand why this voice was continually playing in the background of my life. As I danced around our house with my daughter with a new excitement for living, I finally understood what her song meant.

It's funny what treasures you can find when you open your mind and free your dreams. This song isn't inspirational to me because I dream of becoming a rock star and touring the world. I believe this song was introduced into my life because it speaks to me on a level of thought I can finally understand.

The words and message in this song were precisely what I needed to continue my journey toward fulfillment and happiness. If I didn't change the way I thought about my future, I believe I would never have understood the power and wisdom of this woman's words.

This song has not only become my anthem to push me through moments of doubt and fear but a song I play on repeat every day. It is not a song I would ever have thought I would listen to every day, but the words and energy this song bring me are a gift I cash in every day. When I start to lose faith that my life has already been written in stone, I put on my headphones and press play.

The power and belief I feel from her words give me the strength to see my future as though it is already here. Since I started to write this book, I have found many more songs that give me the strength to fight for my dreams, but this song deserves my appreciation.

Words can't express the gratitude I feel for a twenty-year-old singer-songwriter I have never met. I wouldn't have written this book without her voice pushing me every day to find the man I can finally see. A man who finally understands the power in finding the wild things in life.

There is a wild thing that exists in all of us, it lives in our passions, in the people we love, in our subconscious thought, our beliefs. It's even made a home in the darkest part of us. But we can't be scared of it. We have to become it. — Alessia Cara

Introduction

This book is a personal collection of motivational and inspirational quotes from a young writer without fear of the unknown. The writer is me, and all the quotes in this book are my original quotes. These quotes are not taken from books or writings from the past but inspired by a belief in a power I choose to embrace. They are influenced by my faith in happiness and what is possible when we choose to believe our thoughts can create.

This is a collection of thoughts and quotes I use every day to help me see a world I believe is possible. A world I know is already mine. If you have a dream for a better life but cannot break free from the life you have created, this book will open your mind and soul to a new way of thinking. With each quote in this book, I have written a personal narrative to give you a glimpse into my mind as I read and respond to its direction. Some thoughts in this book are similar only because their simplicity has power. Only you can find the strength to write the next chapter in your life, but I hope my words will give you the courage to seek a life you thought only existed in your dreams.

Join me on my journey toward fulfillment and the life you know you deserve. Only you can find your perfect life, so let this book help you unlock the power and potential of your mind. When you choose to find your purpose and attack your fears, the positivity and gratefulness you create will fuel the belief in your dreams.

Use these words to inspire a new chapter in your life and give birth to the person you know you can become.

Find Your Purpose

Attack your day with purpose, or your purpose will be serving someone else's dreams and desires.

Having a purpose for every day you are on this earth creates the progress needed to construct your dreams and desires. Not just an idea but a step-by-step plan for each day that aligns with your goals and vision for a better life. Don't pretend you can run through your day and make a plan as you tackle daily tasks.

If you have no plan to start your day, you are planning to become an unappreciated contestant in a game you cannot win. You will not be asked to help write the rules, and you will have no input into how this game is constructed. You will only receive a small door prize from the person who was courageous enough to unlock their dreams. If you don't have a purpose for tomorrow, you will become the pawn.

Use this quote to keep you focused on your daily goals so you don't get lost in someone else's vision.

Don't wait for a storm to change your life; create the storm that will change your life.

The power of positive thinking can sometimes get lost in the waves of our daily lives. Our hopes and dreams can lie alone underneath a single-engine boat in the middle of a shallow ocean.

We sit and wait for a gust of wind to take our rusty boat to shore so we can step out and sink our feet deep into the sand. We look around for a lifetime for this limitless wind to attach to our sails and bring us freedom.

If you truly want to change your life and walk with two feet in the sand, you must stop waiting for a gentle breeze and become the storm that will guide you to shore. You must do something every day to create the wind that will turn your boat into a vessel that will guide you to the place you dream of.

Use this quote on the days when your belief in your dreams starts to fade away and you revert to your routine.

Decide what you want in life and tell the world it's yours.

Start today by deciding what you want in life. Write your goals and dreams down on paper. Once you have done this simple and freeing task, you will acquire the direction to attain the happiness that has been removed from your life. You will see the things in life that bring you joy and calmly release yourself from the unhappiness that may surround you.

When you are confident of the life you want to live tomorrow, you must start convincing yourself of its impending inevitability today. You cannot be afraid to tell all those who will nurture your dreams.

You will find that your direction will not only become more apparent, but the ones who believe in you will find ways to join your journey. They will look for different paths that may help you achieve your goals and dreams. Share your ideas and conviction with the ones you love and you will have a team prepared to look for opportunities.

Use this quote on days when you think nothing can stop your dreams from coming to life and share your confidence with your chosen team.

Tonight, I will dream of a better tomorrow, but today I will awake with a vision more ambitious than yesterday.

If you wait to fall asleep to dream, then you are wasting precious time. You need to make it your purpose to dream before your head hits the pillow. Imagine a life that will provide you with the moments that only dreams are made of. It could be something small you want to accomplish or something big you want to experience. Make sure that, before you sleep, you have imagined positive outcomes for the day ahead. You have the power and potential in your mind to create and manipulate how tomorrow will play out.

Make it part of your routine to spend ten minutes before you go to bed visualizing your dreams and goals for tomorrow. Map out your day and visualize positive results. This act will not only give you structure but a heads-up before you hit the pillow.

Use this quote before you go to bed so you can be prepared for what tomorrow will present.

If you don't know who you want to become or the life you want to live, you need to figure that out today or tomorrow will be the same as yesterday.

If you are genuinely ready to change your life, you need to change the way you think. If you are not happy with the person you have become, you need to make it your purpose to create the best version of you. No one can tell you what this looks like or how to find it. You are the only one who can decide the life you want to live in.

Don't worry right now about how that is going to happen. Just be sure in your mind that the person you are crafting is the person you want to become. You can create a new life today, but you first must ask yourself who you want to become.

Use this quote when you are unsure of the person you want to develop, and honestly ask yourself the question.

Since everything in this world is connected, be sure not to live life in a bubble of your creation.

We all have had times in our lives when leaving the house seems unsurmountable or even debilitating. We refuse to answer phone calls and let our emails accumulate to the point where we feel overwhelmed. If you want to have a better life, you need to break free from this bubble.

If you are the only inhabitant inside this sphere, your life will be lonely. Every time you enter this bubble, the walls grow thicker and the people surrounding it will start to move further away.

If you have been fortunate enough to find the perfect life in your mind, you need to free yourself from seclusion. The direction you seek to attain your dreams will come in many forms, but you need to open every line of communication. You need to stay connected to the world that surrounds you because that world will provide answers.

Use this quote when you feel the need to close yourself off from a world that has the answers you seek.

Never try to change a world you don't understand. Change yourself and your world will change with you.

Never attempt to understand the world you live in today. There are so many phenomena you cannot explain, and there are moments that make you wonder why the world always conspires against you. You need to realize that the first step in changing your world starts in your mind and thoughts. You need to take control of your mind before you take control of your life. Once you create the person you want to become in your mind, the world will give you opportunities to transform the life you live into the life you imagine.

Use this quote whenever you cannot understand why bad things always seem to happen in your life.

The light that shines within doesn't have to stay within.

We all have a dream in life that creates an attitude of success that is infectious to anyone who comes into our presence. When we talk about this dream, our passion oozes out of our subconscious with ease. It is never forced because you feel elation with every smile it initiates. Unfortunately, most of us never let this passion stay long enough for it to manifest into reality.

We may let it out for a moment or two, but as soon as negativity and doubt infiltrate our mind, this passion evaporates. Have you ever been so excited about a goal or dream that everyone around you would listen with intent? They could feel a spark in your voice because your conviction was definite. Never let your passions flicker when they radiate the best version of you. Do not let dreams hide when they can create a life surrounded by love. Free your dream and the universe will affirm your intention.

Use this quote when you have a passion in life but never give it a chance to initiate growth.

If the story of your life is in black and white, change the frequency and experience life in color.

We all tell ourselves the perfect story to justify the lives we live in. A perfect and presentable description of why we cannot have the lives we want. The more you tell this story the more believable it becomes. It has great character and a presentable plot, but the reality is something out of an Alfred Hitchcock film. It has no color because you created a horrific ending with no imagination.

Why not tell a story of a life that causes you to jump out from the screen with a new outlook on life? The stories we tell ourselves will become the scripts that guide our future. Make sure your story has a lead character and a closing scene worth the price of admission.

Use this quote when you dare to write a new ending to the story of your life.

Don't invent a new mousetrap; create a new mouse.

Throughout my life, I have spent many business meetings talking about mousetraps and widgets. If you can create a superior product, you have the beginnings of a fortune. What if that product was you? What if you could create a version of you that was superior to the one that exists today? A person with the qualities and characteristics that others wait in line to experience.

With the power of positive thoughts, you can jump straight to the front of the line. Do not get trapped in the cycle of negativity that produced the prototype no one is buying. Make advancements to the prototype and the final product will fly off the shelves.

Use this quote at the beginning of your journey to remember that you need to change before your life changes.

Change your daily habits to give your mind the freedom to create.

Your daily habits need to adjust if you are ready for change. You cannot continue to do the same things you do today and expect different results. If you are looking to change your circumstances, you need to reshape how you live. You cannot continue down the same path you currently walk if you want to live in a place where you dream.

To drastically change your life, you need to change your habits and free your mind. You would not run a marathon without finding the right running shoes. Before you can get to the finish line, you need to understand the steps necessary to attain the stamina to finish the race. Find your dream first, and then create habits to give your mind the freedom to see the finish line.

Use this quote when you have found a goal and are ready to change your habits.

Growing isn't just about the end result; it starts with small steps and daily progress. Make progress every day, and your direction will become clearer.

Always focus on the end result of the vision and dreams you are looking to create. You need to spend an extraordinary amount of time envisioning your dreams as if you already have them. When you believe that they are possible, the direction will come. Although this should be your focus, you should never forget about the daily steps required to help you realize this life. If you have a negative outlook on life and rush through your days without a purpose, you will never be in a state of receiving.

Always have a plan for your day so your thoughts can be proactive and not a reaction to circumstances. Create daily habits to establish the structure needed to develop the necessary steps to accomplish your goals.

Use this quote if you feel you are reverting to your old routine.

Action is not a physical motion but the response to your thoughts.

Taking action is not possible if you do not produce thoughts to proceed with movement. Before your body can move, your mind must decide that it's the right step to take. Once you have inspired thought, you can do one of two things.

You can choose to procrastinate or you can embrace the inner voice that is screaming to proceed. Action is only physical once you respond to your thoughts with decisiveness.

Nothing in life is created without an idea, and nothing is accomplished without effort. These two things are always connected. Make sure not to underestimate the power of your thoughts. If you choose not to respond to your thoughts, the action does not exist. Make sure your thoughts are positive so your responses will move you closer to the vision you have created.

Use this quote when you feel the urge to take action after an inspired thought.

If you look in the mirror and see failure, look again.

This quote came to me during the first day that I realized I needed to change the way I think and the way I choose to live. We all have days when we feel we are not enough. We hesitate to look in the mirror because we are afraid to see the reflection that stares back with disappointment.

This mirror can be in your living room or your mind, but if the reflection is not what you want, look again. Close your eyes, open your mind, and take another look.

The reflection you see is only a reflection today. When you decide to change how you live every day, this reflection will soon transform into affection for the person staring back.

If you do not appreciate who you have become, you need to change how you see yourself. Your image can be changed when you decide to look at the reflection of your future self and live in this reality. See success in your reflection, and you will reflect the confidence that will deliver results.

Use this quote when you think you have failed and understand that your reflection is how you choose to respond.

A thousand wishes unasked are worth nothing, but one dream surrounded by passion and purpose is powerful beyond belief.

Have you ever dreamed of a genie who would appear in your darkest days in a haze of happenstance? A mystical figure who could provide you with three wishes that would change your life. It's a pretty unfulfilling dream when you know the genie only exists in a children's book. But how about if you believed in this genie with the innocence and conviction of a developing child?

Imagine if you had access to a genie who could grant any wish you could create in your mind. It may be hard to imagine, but what if this was possible? You would spend weeks coming up with the perfect wish and spend months crafting its outcome. It would become an essential aspect of your life because you accepted its inevitability.

If you had one wish in life, would you ask for more wishes or would you ask for exactly what you want? One dream surrounded with passion, purpose, and belief will release a power you thought only existed in a fairy tale.

Use this quote whenever you think your wishes will never be answered.

Don't cast judgment until you are willing to judge yourself.

On your journey toward your new life, you will have many people stare at you with skepticism and tell you the life you want is impossible. They will say you don't have the money, you are not smart enough, or your goals are unrealistic. In their minds, they do not believe that your goals and dreams are possible. They cannot see a path to obtain these unrealistic goals you have decided you can achieve. They may have never gone after their dreams because of this mentality or have tried, failed, and given up. Remember that they have never been given the gift of a positive mind, and not too long ago, you were wrapped up in that same empty box. Judge yourself first, and let the universe judge your actions.

Use this quote when you tell a friend your goals and they look at you with skepticism.

The eyes of a leader can be seen in all those who decide to listen and believe their goals are attainable.

Leadership skills have become an excellent characteristic for your resume. It has such a narrow connotation that most believe it is a trait held by someone in a corner office. Leadership is not about how much money you make or how many people you control.

You can make millions of dollars a year and manage dozens of employees, but that does not qualify you as a leader. It may put you in a position with a beautiful view, but great leaders are not given people to follow them; they create ideas and direction that invite followers. They decide that what they see is attainable and they believe in success despite obstacles.

Leadership skills should not be a tagline to a resume if you believe you can lead. Leadership is not about acquiring the herd but being able to listen when the dogs are barking. Your vision, combined with your ability to listen intently, will create a pasture where you can lead with your eyes wide open.

Use this quote when you think you lack leadership skills.

Don't reach out to me if you want to talk about the disappointment of yesterday. Only wake me if you are willing to attack today and I will be by your side.

This quote came to me after a conversation with a friend who was going through some difficult times. After a spirited and candid conversation, I demanded my friend stop feeling sorry for himself and start making the necessary changes. I told him not to call me until he had made the progress we had discussed.

It might be a hard conversation to have with yourself or the ones you love, but sometimes it must be had. If you believe someone is ready to change the way they think about life, show them a direction they may not be able to find. Show them a path that can transform their thoughts into actions and their dreams into reality. This quote will also help you fight the internal battle you will face between the two voices on either side of depression.

Use this quote when you start to talk about and discuss the disappointment of yesterday.

Every morning, when you open your eyes and embrace your passion, encourage yourself never to fall asleep again.

Every morning you have a choice: awake to the sound of an alarm clock or awake with a purpose. I fight every morning never to hear an alarm that has no idea of what I need to accomplish during my day. I refuse to listen to the sound of defeat before I taste my morning coffee. I decide to wake every day with ambition. I choose a vision for my future that I can see as soon as I open my eyes.

No matter how many hours I have slept, I know that when I wake, I am prepared and ready to attack my day. I'm not afraid to fall asleep because I'm prepared to give everything I have when I rise. My dreams have become so bright in my mind that I fight every morning to see an alarm clock that makes no sound.

Use this quote before you go to bed and every time your alarm clock tells you that you are not prepared.

If you think that life is not worth living, create a new life.

Throughout our lives, situations and circumstances can create a depression that seems to control our days and make us give up on ourselves. This feeling can take us away from the people we love and forge an image of ourselves that is disgusting. An image that is not worth living. It can create a feeling of failure and extinguish the flickering light we call life.

Life is too short to live in regret. If you're not completely happy with the life you live, take solace in the fact that you are the creator of your life. If the life you live in today is unexciting, decide to create a new life that you can accept.

Once you realize that tomorrow can be magnificent, you will manufacture a life worth living.

Use this quote when you are at a low point in your life and you are ready for change.

Darkness is not the absence of light; it's the absence of a purpose.

We all have days when nothing goes right and we are unsure of how we will ever have the things in life that make us happy. You feel lost in your daily struggles and feel you will never be able to break free from the life that is causing you so much stress and disappointment. The simple answer is you haven't decided what you want in life or given yourself a purpose to get up every day.

The more complex side of this darkness is you feel life is insignificant and not under your control. You have a choice to find a purpose that will create a light to ignite your passion.

If you think that darkness lasts forever, set your imaginary alarm clock and watch a sunrise with a smile on your face. Force it if you must. Every day we have an opportunity to create something better. Once you find a purpose in life, the darkness you see will dissipate into the light.

Use this quote when you think darkness will forever surround your life and choose to watch your dream smile through the darkness.

Strengthen your body so your mind has a place to live when you attack your day.

For your mind to function at full capacity, it will need a solid foundation to grow and subsist. You need to incorporate some physical activity into your day. This might seem like a lot of work at first, but the benefits will be twofold.

If going to the gym is not an option, then spend fifteen minutes every morning taking a walk before you shower. Not only will your body start to regenerate, but your mind will have newfound energy to attack your day.

Your body and your mind must be at one and connected if you want your dreams to thrive. Insert physical activity into your daily routine. You will not only feel stronger but also more energized to fight off the negative images that will try to attack your mind.

Use this quote every morning when you feel like skipping your exercise routine.

Raise the standards of how you live today to free the person you know you can become tomorrow.

If your standard of life is unsuitable, raise the standards of how you live. There is a reason why you live the life you have today. There is no one to blame but yourself if the life you have created is mediocre. Don't continue to do the same things you did yesterday if you want different results tomorrow.

If you're going to create the best version of yourself, raise your standards to mirror the person you admire most. If you want to lose weight, get moving; if you're going to write a best-selling book, open your laptop and start punching keys. We can all see the person we want to become but never make the necessary changes needed to become that individual. Don't be afraid of hard work. Raise your standards to give birth to your future self.

Use this quote when you have a resolution and always seem to fall short.

Do what makes you happy or do nothing.

This quote may be hard to grasp because we all have daily tasks that need respect. I'm not saying you should forget about the things that provide for your family. This quote is about the time you have left. If you want to experience life as the best version of yourself, you need to do what makes you happy. Providing for your family deserves respect, but so do your dreams.

Make sure you have a dedicated plan in place every day that brings you closer to the vision you have created. Nothing in life is given to you, but you can choose to take control of the time you have. If you cannot find happiness, make time to find it. Only you know what makes you happy.

Never let your dreams fade away with a desire to pay your bills.

Use this quote when you are too focused on work and do not give yourself the time to follow your dreams.

Happiness is easy to obtain when you decide what happy is.

People define happiness in many different forms, and it's never the same for every person. True happiness does not come easy, nor does it have a dollar value. The definition of happiness is yours to create, and you will not find it in a book because you must be the author. You must decide what happiness means to you. Do not let anyone define your joy when they cannot understand your hopes and dreams.

Have you ever really sat down and put serious thought into what makes you happy? The things in life that make your smile permanent. Once you truly understand what makes you happy, you will start to approach the life you always imagined was possible. We all have a murky vision of happiness in our minds but never find the clarity to seek its reality. Decide what makes you smile and believe the path will present itself. Only then will you obtain true happiness.

Use this quote when you are ready to sit down and ask yourself what makes you happy.

If someone could give you everything you wanted in life by giving you one simple formula, would you walk away or walk with purpose?

The ideas in this book are not new and you may be doing some of them every day. You may be great at one but don't follow the others. You may give your time to a charity every weekend but not tell the people in your life how grateful you are for their support. You may have a great routine to start your day but once your day gets off track have no skills to retrain your mind to recapture your vision. I have incorporated some of these principles in part over the last five years but always found a way to revert to my old ways.

Once you realize all these actions are a part of something bigger, you will start to make it your purpose to follow its direction. When you have a greater understanding of the power in these actions, you will see the formula has relevance.

Use this quote when you question the power of a positive purpose.

Attack Your Fears

Always be willing to embrace the moment when the power of belief overtakes your fear of failure.

There are certain moments during your day that provide completely contrasting paths. The first path has very few obstacles or obstructions. It is a nice, leisurely walk toward comfort and familiarity. You have walked this path a thousand times before, so to walk it again is effortless. You know exactly where the road ends. The second path, however, is not natural, and the terrain feels very discomforting. Once you convert your fears into positive outcomes, the second path will become the only option. Be willing to walk the latter path when the belief in your dreams starts to overpower your fear of failure. When you understand that fear doesn't slow your journey, you will be prepared to embrace its potential for growth.

Use this quote at any moment you feel doubt and understand that fear is a path that contains the answers you need to grow.

Fear is not real when you decide it is only in your mind.

The power of fear can be felt from the deepest parts of your stomach to the most unfamiliar parts of your mind. It can only survive and break your will because you choose to see its negative personality.

When you start to see fear as a tool and not a limitation, you will understand the real power and potential it can possess. The physical reaction to fear can be real, but once you realize how to control and respond to its instruction, you will welcome its magnetism.

Use this quote in the moments when you feel fear during your day and remind yourself that only you create fear and that you can control its direction.

If a person's mind is not free of fear, can a person see clearly enough to be a witness to his or her own decisions?

When fear becomes the deciding factor in how you make decisions, you will witness freedom or experience defeat.

You need to control how you respond to the fear you face every day. Fear can drive you out of your comfort zone if you decide to put two hands on the wheel. It can control how many red lights you see as the traffic starts to clutter your mind. When you free yourself from the fears you face in life, your decisions will become clearer.

Fear can guide our choices. If you do not know why you feel fear you will never be present when you need its direction. Be a witness to what it represents and understand that it can provide you with the green light to put your foot on the gas. Only you can embrace fear, and only you can decide who sits behind the wheel.

Use this quote when you start to make a decision based on fear so you can reevaluate what drives your choices.

Your wildest dreams are only a thought away once you unlock the mind that holds your doubt.

An impossible dream does not have to live at a distance if you believe it is possible. When you decide that the fear you feel every day holds the key to your deepest desires, you will understand. Once you let your dreams overpower your doubt, your mind will be free to unlock the door to the place where your idea has been left to die.

You may not see it today, but if you look carefully and intently through this hollow door, you will see that your dream is still breathing.

From a distance, it may be surrounded in darkness, but once you start to take small steps toward your dream, it will begin to rise from the dark and doubt will disappear. With every positive thought you inject into your mind your dream gains strength. With positivity and belief, you will soon be ready to take the next step.

Use this quote when you have a dream that has been gasping for a new beginning.

If you feel fear on your journey, you are on the right path.

Fear is such a powerful emotion that most of us choose to let it control every aspect of our lives. It can be so pronounced you can feel its weakening as sickness. Fear is not only powerful, but it can be immobilizing.

It can make us drop to our knees and throw in the towel before we step into the ring. We see fear as defeat and not as a direction. When you realize fear is an opportunity, you will understand that holding the towel close will create the sweat needed to accomplish any goal.

If you feel fear, be thankful that you can feel something. Once you understand that fear is not your opponent but your cut man, you will lace up the gloves with confidence. You will be ready to put in the hard work necessary to see life with poise to knock out any obstacle entering your ring.

Use this quote when you are ready to attack your fears and face any obstacle that stands in your way.

One of the greatest gifts in life is knowing that your gift should never live in silence.

Do you excel at something in life but cannot see a future where that could provide you with financial freedom? We all need to pay our bills and put food on the table, so we choose to spend our time doing things that will make this possible. This is not a failure by any means; it's a noble act to provide for your family.

What if you could find a world where your greatest passion was your career? You would not only put food on the table but live every day with a full plate. If you have a passion in life, you cannot store it on a shelf that no one can find, in the back of a pantry, where no one can see it.

Give it a voice every day and embrace the freedom and joy it will create. Life is not just about the necessities but about abundance. It is necessary to do the things you love if you seek the ingredients to prepare a life that will leave you satisfied.

Use this quote when you have a passion that you choose to silence.

For anyone to see their future, they must be willing to put the past behind them while understanding the power and opportunity that is created from failure.

Your past can thrust you toward the life you have always wanted or hold your dreams in a bubble that cannot be broken. To see the future, you must create a mind that understands failure is knowledge. You cannot succeed without failure, and you cannot burst the bubble without understanding the opportunity failure creates.

When you fail in life, you cannot stop searching for different ways to accomplish your goals. One failure can create multiple opportunities to see different paths. You must be willing to see the opportunity failure creates and not its manufactured ending. If your past failures hold you back from accomplishing your goals of tomorrow, prepare yourself for future failures.

Put the past behind you, but always be thankful for the knowledge and opportunities failure produces. Your past is a great engine to guide your goals of tomorrow when you see it as opportunities and not as roadblocks.

Use this quote when you look to the past for reasons why failure is a part of your future.

Never be afraid to reach for the stars, but don't forget to hold on to your vision as you choose to rise above others' expectations.

Fear is one of the most powerful emotions you will experience. It can motivate or destroy any dream you can conceive. One thing to learn from this book is that you cannot let fear stop you from going after the things you desperately desire. No matter how you choose to rise above others' small-minded thinking, make sure you hold your vision in high regard.

Choose to see the vision you have created and keep it clear in your mind. Others' expectations of success do not have to be your reality. There are people around you today who will have trouble believing you can achieve greatness. Do not let them tell you that your star cannot be reached. Don't be afraid to go after the biggest dream you can imagine when your vision is the expectation you believe is worth holding.

Use this quote when others tell you that your dreams will never be reached.

Your greatest defeat is your greatest opportunity to understand that defeat is powerful.

Defeat is a requirement for anyone who ever created something unbelievable. Failure can be demoralizing to anyone with superficial hope that they will accomplish their goals. It can, however, be a powerful motivator for those who have an unwavering belief that their dreams are undeniable.

It is essential to understand that failure happens to everyone who dreams big. It is how you choose to use its direction that will ultimately decide if your dreams are indisputable. Never have an adverse reaction to defeat; use it as an opportunity to learn and understand its power and perspective. If one path did not give you the desired results, realize you are much closer to your goal because the way has been vetted. You now have a more definite direction to accomplish your goals.

Use this quote after you experience a failed attempt to achieve your goal.

We all have twenty-four hours in a day, so never use time as an excuse for failure. Failure is not using the time we are given.

I thought of this quote after I told myself that all the things I wanted in life weren't possible because I didn't have enough time to make them happen. After saying this to myself, I started to think of some of the most successful entrepreneurs and leaders I respected. After coming up with about ten names, I asked myself what I had in common with these inspirational leaders. Surprisingly I did have a few traits in common with these great minds, but what resonated was time.

We all have the time to chase our dreams and goals, but most of us use our time to find excuses for why we have no time. When you give your excuses strength, your dreams will not develop, and you will never give yourself the time needed to succeed. The glaring truth is you have the time to accomplish any goal if you believe time is not an obstacle. Give your attention to your dreams and not time.

Use this quote when you feel the urge to sit back and relax when you have a clear vision of your future.

Do not look for success through an open door. Open the door where your deepest fear lies and you will find everything you need.

We all look for success through the narrow lens that we have created. We can see that promotion because we walk by the door to our new office every day. You can picture yourself sitting in your ergonomically designed chair, staring out through the window of your newly furnished office.

You propel yourself into this new world because you believe that it is possible. You have the means to see its outcome daily. If this picture is all you can see, it will be all you will possibly receive. To find the success and happiness you truly desire, you must be willing to look past the open door. Embrace the fear that lies behind the door you have been afraid to open. Decide you can have more than the life you created and use fear as your guide to what you truly desire.

Use this quote when your path to success has limited options without the possibility of making you feel completely fulfilled.

Don't hide from fear; do one thing every day that will drive your fear into hiding.

Make it your purpose every day to face your fears. Do not hide when you feel fear in the pit of your stomach, but actively search for opportunities to look fear in the eyes. Even if you are afraid to admit it, there are things you fear in life and try to avoid at all costs. You will find whatever excuse you can to hide from its intimidation.

When you choose to overcome your fears and control the emotions they introduce, you will find that fear is inferior to the power you possess. Write down your top ten fears in life and make it your mission to start crossing them off your list. One by one, you will realize your biggest fear is the face staring back in your reflection.

Use this quote to understand you must not hide from fear but embrace the freedom it can give you.

To change your world, you need to unleash the caged voice you have been afraid to free.

Have you ever heard a voice in your head you dismissed as a crazy thought? Have you ever had a dream that everyone said was impossible? To change your world into the vision you now hold firmly in your mind, that voice needs to be uncaged.

You must unlock the power of this voice and reimagine the cage to give you the freedom to rumble. Your negativity and doubt created the cage that exists and it's now used as the foundation of your thoughts. Change your thoughts and this voice will be free from any cage created by man.

You must understand that once you change your negative persona into a more positive and productive version of yourself, the gates will open with opportunities to roar. The cage may be locked today, but the key is in your possession.

You have spent your entire life in a cage of your creation, and only you can rip down the walls with ferocity. The voice you have been afraid to free has the potential to turn a whimper into a roar if you believe the cage doesn't exist.

Use this quote during your day when you choose to dismiss the voice that refuses to live in the cage you created.

Choose Positivity

When you have the perfect vision of your future, hold it in your thoughts like it is the last breath you will ever take.

It may take time to really see the perfect vision of your future. It may come to you in an instant or it may develop over your transformation toward a more positive mind. When you find the vision that becomes the picture you see every day, you need to breathe deeply. The image you have found will provide you with an unlimited supply of clean air. Exhale the negativity you have been holding deep in your mind so you can filter the thoughts that bring purity. Decide what your perfect life looks like and keep the vision in your mind. Imagine the feelings of already having attained the life you want. Hold this vision in your thoughts with absolute certainty. If you are drowning in your current life and gasping for hope, you need to breathe the freshness of positivity and belief.

Use this quote when you have the perfect vision of the life you want to attain so you can hold it fresh in your mind every day.

You hold the key to unlock any dream you can conceive when you understand the power you possess in your subconscious mind.

We all have a power that exists in our minds. We can change our thoughts in an instant and change our circumstances for eternity. Your mind holds the answers to your happiness. You can decide today to use your mind to unlock your dreams of a better life. It is your choice of what thoughts you let into your mind, so make sure you choose wisely.

Every thought you hold in your mind has power. If it stays long enough it can bring you joy, and it can also bring pain. You must be fully aware of your thoughts and find ways to control what opinions you hold. When you have the dedicated discipline to think positive thoughts and beliefs predominantly, you will have the power to predict your future.

Use this quote if you underestimate the power of positive thinking and the influence your mind must create.

When the clouds pretend to block out the sun, remember that the sun is still shining.

On your journey toward a positive outlook on life, you are going to have mornings when you feel the excitement of living. You will arrive at work with the confidence only seen in the top one percent. Then, in a blink of an eye, something will happen that will knock you to the bottom of the pack. When this happens, you need to know that your dreams and goals are still in the same place you left them. They may be hard to find when you let negative thoughts enter your mind, but they still have influence.

No matter what small obstacle has entered your day, you must hit back with 99 percent of your mind. Never let the little things block out the vision you have been fighting so hard to keep. Your goals are still shining if you refuse to let obstacles cloud your vision. Surround your vision with sunshine and the clouds will only be an illusion.

Use this quote in the mornings when you feel you are making progress but one small obstacle takes away your thunder.

If you don't believe in the power of positive thinking, you are absolutely right.

Once you say the words, "It can't be done," you might as well move on to the next empty dream at the bottom of your wish list. This negative mentality will crush any idea you have and leave it buried underneath doubt and uncertainty. Use the power of belief to be sure you will accomplish your goals and dreams. If you have no feeling behind your goals, they will never have the strength needed to exist. When you carry negative thoughts to the place where you dream, the dream will die. You might as well dig the grave yourself and write a mesmerizing eulogy about potential. When you attach a positive thought to your dreams, you will become a disciple in position to watch your dream rise from the dead.

Use this quote when you think positive thinking is a waste of time because you have no control over what happens in life.

The world can cast a shadow over any person who is not willing to embrace opportunity.

Once you have a positive outlook on life, opportunity can be found around any corner. You cannot embrace an opportunity if you live in a shadow of fear and doubt. If you are not prepared to search for opportunities to accomplish your goals, you will only find darkness. You first need to prepare your mind and change your perception of what is possible. Once you have belief in your goals, opportunities will emerge. If you choose to ignore the opportunities that will bring you closer to your goals, you will never be able to walk out of the shadows. When an opportunity presents itself as direction, you must drive fear and doubt into submission and act. There can be no shadow without the presence of light, so make sure you are standing in the right position.

Use this quote when you are afraid to chase an opportunity that will get you closer to your goal.

When you let your dreams crawl underneath depression, you will never find the peace you desire.

The greatest battle I have faced on my journey is the fight I face every day to capture my negative thoughts and release them from my mind. You cannot run from the depression that your negative thoughts establish. Accept that they are normal and understand that they can be replaced. Never let your dark days suffocate the light you fight every day to keep you warm. A mind that is in a constant state of depression will imprison any hope you have for peace. You need to find ways to capture your negative thoughts when depression is your cellmate.

If you want the peace you desire, you must fight the depression with the force of a thousand positive thoughts. Your dreams cannot live in a mind that is dominated by depression. You must decide how you want to live out your remaining days. Replace your negative thoughts with the belief in your dreams so you can peacefully judge your decisions.

Use this quote on the mornings when you cannot fight the depression that is gaining strength.

Demand your mind to be in a good state when you feel the hand of doubt crawling down your spine.

The doubt you feel today is understandable, and I feel its hand every day. It can grab me by the neck with two hands as it tries to sink its dirty nails deep into my mind. When you start to feel its grip, you need to turn your head and look into its eyes forcefully. Once you face your doubts with positive thoughts, they will release their hold one hand at a time. Every time you replace uncertainty with belief, your mind will be free to grab the biggest dream you can conceive. You must fight the doubt you feel every day with the knowledge that your dreams are possible. When you feel doubt, it is a signal that you need to change the way you are thinking at that moment.

Use this quote anytime you have doubts that your dreams can become a reality.

Darkness surrounds your life, and so does happiness—you choose.

We all have the choice to be happy or depressed. I understand that some situations need to be controlled, but make no mistake that the choice is yours. We all have days that make us unwilling to face the world. You need to find the strength to choose the happiness that surrounds you. I understand that the darkness is real and it has control of your life. I'm not ignorant of the power it can have over your life because I have seen its face. You need to realize that you do have a choice.

I know of a power that may be hard to believe but comes with a freedom that will be felt by everyone who surrounds you. You are not only strong enough to see the light, but you can choose happiness when the sun starts to set. Never underestimate the power of a positive mind and what you can control. You are surrounded with happiness, but only you can find a way to let it shine in the darkest days.

Use this quote when you choose to let depression control your day and cannot see the beauty that surrounds your life.

When you get angry about a bad situation, it eliminates your ability to overcome its negativity.

We build up so much negativity over our lives that it seems reasonable to give it creditability. Every negative thought you accept is a barrier to the growth you are attempting to create. Once you have decided to let positivity be the blueprint, you need to fight the anger and release the negativity that has been controlling your life.

Many days you will have anger that will test your new mindset—moments that will eliminate any hope you have for a better life. This anger reduces your ability to live a life you dream is possible. You need to find ways to overcome its influence.

Anger is not your friend; it is an emotion you need to control as you work toward a new positive mind. When you feel anger enter your mind, stop and reevaluate why it exists.

Your anger is only present because your mind is not strong enough to understand its existence. You may think the anger is out of your control, but when you decide not to give it strength, you will become stronger. You will have the ability to control its influence.

Use this quote when you feel anger creep into your consciousness and understand the negative impact it has on your goals.

The greatest gift I have ever received is a knowledge that my wishes are heard every day by a power I can't understand.

If you don't understand how something works, you can still reap the benefits of its functionality. We don't know how many things we use every day actually work. When you turn on a light switch, do you really know how that action brings you light? You probably have no idea how electricity works, but you do know that when you flick the switch, you see the light. You do not question its reality but only benefit from its creation.

When you use this same mindset to see your future, you will understand the gift of belief and positive thinking. Your wishes will be heard if you have the courage and conviction to turn on the light that has been in darkness. You may not agree with some of the principles in this book, but you can choose to control your thoughts and feel the energy a positive mind can generate. You do not need to understand how it works, but you can flick the switch and electrify your mind.

Use this quote when you have a hard time understanding the power of belief.

The future can sometimes be seen before we are willing to accept its inevitability.

Once you have found the perfect vision of your future, you need to spend dedicated time during your day picturing yourself living your dream. Envision yourself starting your new business, cooking in your new kitchen, or walking hand in hand with your new love. You need to witness your future before you accept direction. You may not honestly believe it today, but every day you choose to propel yourself into your dream, you will start to think it's possible. Fight every day to see the life you have always dreamed of and the path will be presented. Your acceptance of its inevitability must be absolute.

Use this quote during times when you lack faith in your vision.

When you open a book, expect to see words. When you open your mind and free your thoughts, expect to see a world that you deserve.

Reading books is an integral part of your journey, but make sure you are reading the right books. When you open a book, you do not expect to see empty pages. You are positive that words will be the first thing you see. Once you open your mind to a life of positivity, you should anticipate higher expectations.

We all have predictions of a life we can accomplish. It might be the life our parents envisioned for us or a job that a friend said would provide for our family. These are noble paths you can take, but what about the book that was never written and the book that has an unknown author and a story that has never been told? You have the power to create any story you choose to write. You do not have to buy the book that has been written by the masses if you decide to become the author.

Use this quote when you feel the only options you have are the ones that have been presented as plausible.

When someone tells you it can't be done, remind them it is already here.

On your journey, you will encounter many people who will always remind you that your dreams are too big. They will inform you that the possibility of accomplishing your goals is unlikely. You need to keep these people at a distance, but if they do declare their views, make sure you keep your vision sharp. Let them know your goals and dreams are real because you refuse to see a different outcome. The only result you see is the vision you work so hard to devise.

Do not let your hard work be taken away by someone who doesn't understand the power of your positive mind. Let them continue their journey toward mediocrity while you turn your thoughts into results. They can continue to see life under a microscope while you fight to create a lab prepared to construct your hypothesis.

Use this quote when someone tries to explain your dreams with a hypothesis that has no power.

There is beauty in every moment once you open your mind and experience the power of clarity.

So many moments in your day are absolutely beautiful and breathtaking. Once you understand the power of positive thinking, these moments will be frequently witnessed. You will start to view the world with a different mindset, and the sunset you briefly looked at yesterday will become a moment you will cherish as the moon smiles in the distance. When you decide to smile back with a clear vision of your future, you will feel the power clarity can create. Once you become one with your goals and your dreams, the universe will help you experience life in a luminous simplicity.

The answers exist in the world that surrounds your life. You need to be completely clear about the goals you wish to accomplish. Decide what experience you want to live and your direction will become a combination of the warmth of the sun and the mystery of the moon.

Use this quote when you have found the perfect vision of your future and seek inspiration to find clarity and direction.

A good head on your shoulders is great for photographs, but a positive mind is perfectly positioned to create a bigger and brighter picture.

This quote came to me after a conversation with my mother as I explained my new way of thinking and my desire to write my first book. As I proceeded to tell her that I was going to sell five hundred thousand copies of this book, she hesitated. "You have a good head on your shoulders," she said. I paused for a second and said this quote. I believe she used those particular words because, like most people, she has been trained to picture a world with limitations and modest expectations.

I do not fault my mom for thinking this way because she was never instructed to grip the camera. She was told to hold a wallet-sized portrait of what is possible. I know my mother believes in my dreams, and her support has given me the strength to fight for my dreams. I believe my words will provide my family with a life-sized portrait of what is possible when you choose to be the photographer.

Use this quote when the ones you love are searching for reasons to believe in your dream but have a hard time seeing the bigger picture.

Control your thoughts; control your emotions; control your future.

This is a sequence you must learn to master if you wish to capture the life you imagine. Controlling your thoughts is about making sure you are equipped to stomp out any negative thoughts that may enter your mind.

They will come in bunches, but you must have a plan prepared to fight them off with a fiery storm of possibility. Once you are in a state of positive thinking, you will be given different paths to harness the gifts you were given at birth.

If you don't know what gifts you possess, think harder. Think about what makes you happy and you will soon start to realize a gift that has been silenced for too long. We all have skills that can create a better future, but you first must understand that you have ultimate control.

Use this quote when negative thoughts enter your mind and tell you that you are inferior.

To be successful, you must surround yourself with a successful vision. Only then should you surround yourself with success.

One of the most important things I have learned since I opened my eyes to a new way of thinking is surrounding myself with successful people; individuals who have already accomplished what I am crafting and understand the power of positive thoughts. However, you should only look for these people when your vision is clear and concise. You may be tempted to look for these individuals at the beginning of your journey, but be careful not to be premature in your thinking.

If you don't have a clear vision or purpose as to what you truly want to accomplish in life, you must wait. To take advantage of surrounding yourself with successful leaders, you must first become positive in your thoughts and the belief that your vision is imminent. Once you have a strong and undeniable vision, you will be competently positioned to take advice and direction.

Use this quote when you are attempting to gain knowledge or advice from someone you admire.

When you decide to take control of your mind, you will take control of your future.

Never disregard how powerful and persuasive your thoughts can be when you are experimenting with a positive mindset. Everything in life first must be constructed in your mind. You must take control of the pictures you create and be completely conscious of what thoughts you hold in your mind. You must see the image in perfect resolution and without apprehension. The most influential tool we have at our disposal is our minds, and if we don't manipulate them daily, we will never have the power to perceive perfection. Taking control of your mind is about finding ways to overcome negative thoughts and replacing them with your future state of success. Once you find ways to turn pessimism into confidence quickly, your mind will be positioned to receive direction.

Use this quote when you feel a negative thought enter your mind so you can quickly decide to replace it with optimism.

Embrace the warmth of one positive thought to quickly see a light with the power and potential to be illuminated by one simple smile.

It might seem like your dreams are taking a while to come to life, but stay the course and continue to smile every day. Control your thoughts the moment you rise and find something in your life that can make you smile immediately. If you can't think of anything, manufacture a smile until one becomes genuine. If you want to embrace the power of positive thinking, you must be happy. You need to search for ways to smile every day so your dreams can move you forward. If one positive thought can manufacture a single smile, make it a purpose to find this thought and what it represents.

Use this quote when you cannot find the strength to smile during your day.

Happiness is the key to open a door you must walk through to obtain your hopes and dreams.

If you live in a world surrounded by doubt and depression, you will never find a place where you dream. Your hopes and dreams can be a reality if you choose to live life with happiness that infects the world around you. Once you have a positive outlook on life, you will have positive results.

Joy is not only infectious, it is crucial if you are looking for ways to obtain your goals. You will never find the answers or the direction to achieve your goals if you spend your days drowning in self-pity and doubt. Never lock the door from the inside unless you are willing to stay locked in a room without the opportunity to open a window.

Use this quote to understand the importance happiness creates as you chase your dreams.

When the grass looks greener, and the sky seems smaller, your eyes are becoming a part of your journey.

You will observe many things on your journey toward happiness and fulfillment. Once you start to see the life you want as impending, you will begin to see things differently. The surroundings that you have been choosing to ignore will now look abnormal because you have a unique perspective. Use positivity as a replacement for yesterday's negative thoughts and the sky will open with possibility.

The cold and damp rain you ran from yesterday will provide warmth to stand and appreciate the sun. You will need to be completely conscious on your journey toward a more positive mind.

Everything is interconnected, and when your eyes start to notice the beauty that surrounds your life, you will be closer to the peace you desire. Your eyes may be open as you experience nature, but you must make sure you train your eyes to see the beauty in every season.

Use this quote anytime you are at one with nature or taking a walk through a beautiful landscape.

Never let anyone diminish your dreams when they can't understand the power you possess.

On your path, you will come across moments and situations that will make you question your new way of thinking. You will encounter friends and other people thousands of miles away from the positivity you have been fighting so hard to retain. Although they may be looking out for your best interests, they might never understand the power a positive mind can possess. They can only see a future that exists in their mind.

When you let others put doubt and fear in your mind, you are giving them the power to control your future. Everyone has the right to see life with ceilings and limitations, but never let anyone diminish the hard work you put in every day. The power you now possess will give you all you have ever imagined if you distance yourself from negativity.

Use this quote when anyone tells you your new way of thinking is fool's gold.

Each decision we make will guide us down a gravel road surrounded by fear or a path perfectly paved with our desires.

Daily decisions should never be an afterthought but decisive resolutions to positive thoughts. Our choices not only frame our current existence but give us the power to picture our future. During the day, you make thousands of decisions. Big or small, these decisions are guiding you to a future only you can produce. How you see the path is your choice. Will your decisions of tomorrow be the same as yesterday or will your belief pave a path you can walk with purpose and conviction?

We all have a choice in how our lives turn out, and we all have a say in what paths we take. If you take the path surrounded in fear, then fear is what you will find. If you decide to walk the path surrounded by positivity, you will find a purpose.

Use this quote when you are faced with a decision that is tied to your vision.

Breaking through bad days is a skill, and if you don't learn to master it, you will be forever broken.

Bad days are inevitable. They will come often and they will have strength. When you choose to have a positive mindset about life, you will have great days and ones when you wish you could crawl back into bed. You need to be ready for these evil days and be prepared to break the frequency with which they occur. We all have bad days, and we all have moments when we feel like giving up on our dreams. Are you prepared for these moments? You need to develop a skill set for the days you feel dejected. You need to find ways to overcome negative moments during your day and bring yourself back to the vision you have erected. It could be a motivational song or a call to a loved one. You will begin to maximize your potential once you find ways to master the days you feel doubt.

Use this quote when you think bad days cannot be controlled.

The future is a question only one person can answer and create.

If you think that your peers control your future, you must ask yourself if you are surrounding yourself with the right people. Only you can create the life you have always imagined, and no one can answer a question that was never asked. If you do not know the life you want to create, then ask yourself the question. The answers you seek cannot be presented until you ask the question. You can accomplish any goal if you dare to answer this question.

When you finally have the answer, you need to spend every free moment doing something that will question why you waited so long. Your future should not be surrounded by question marks but created by the belief that your dreams will be answered. Only you can question your current life and justify your answer.

Use this quote when you are surrounded by too many question marks.

Be Grateful and Give

When you give something back every day, the universe will understand your dreams and desires.

If you haven't figured out how important giving back is to your journey toward a better life, do something today to feel its power. Your mind will not be working at full capacity if your circumstances limit your ability to give back. When you perceive time and money as limitations to your charity, that will be the story you tell to provide validation. The world around you will start to show answers to your dreams if you are willing to use a small part of your day giving something back. It may be advice given to a lifelong friend or a cup of coffee delivered to a stranger. Once you search for moments in your day to give back, you will not only find peace but create different paths to achieve your goals.

Use this quote after you have chosen to give something back so you have a better understanding of how it will guide your vision.

Tell the ones you love that you are grateful for their support and you will discover a gift that will fuel success.

If you truly want the success you desire, then it's possible. When you tell the ones you love that you are grateful for their support, your dreams will gain energy. Once you have your vision of the perfect life, you must show appreciation to the ones who are helping you achieve the success that you imagine. Every time you say thanks, you are initiating a plan to control your future and your dreams. You will discover a gift that others may not understand but a power that you will embrace.

Use this quote when you underestimate the importance of telling the ones you love that their support is crucial to your success.

Use love and gratefulness every day to get rid of pain and fear.

Love is a powerful emotion that can overpower any negative thought, and gratefulness will keep negativity at bay. Pain and fear are a part of life and will always be present, but they can be minimized. When anxiety and fear creep into your thoughts, you have a choice as to how long they will stay. By controlling your thoughts and emotions, you will control intensity. Love cannot be touched, but if you hold on to its vigor long enough, the pain will have nowhere to lay its ugly head. Pain and fear are a vital part of life because without them we would never be able to appreciate the love that surrounds our lives. Be grateful for the life you have and embrace the love you have found every day.

Use this quote when you feel pain so you can minimize its effect on your emotions.

Saying thank you should never be reactive but always a proactive thought and action.

If you don't think that saying thank you is an explosive act you need to reevaluate your life. If you take advice or support from someone without saying thank you, shame on you for missing this opportunity. If you have a chance to say thank you or be grateful for the support, take advantage. If you think it means nothing, try to remember the last time someone said thank you for a job well done. It needs to become a daily activity.

Search for opportunities throughout your day to say thank you. Make it a purpose in your day to say thank you as many times as you can. It could be excellent service at your favorite restaurant or saying thank you to a colleague for an idea that increased production. Search for moments to say thank you, and you will feel the power of my words. Use this quote to find opportunities to say thank you during your day.

Start your day by saying thank you for the life you have been given and you will be given a gift that you will soon believe is possible.

No matter what your circumstances are today, I can guarantee that something in your life deserves gratitude. As I write these words, I am thankful that I can see the beautiful rolling landscape behind dozens of calming waves. I'm even grateful for the old weathered picnic table where I have placed my laptop as I continue to find these words. Your life may not be perfect, but never forget to say thank you for the experience you have. This must be a daily action you incorporate into your routine.

Once this becomes routine, you will start to understand what impact this has on your mood and your vision for a better life. The power you think doesn't exist in your life can provide you with the ability to capture the life you imagine, but you must be thankful. When you believe in the power of positive thinking, you should not only start your day by saying thank you for the life you have but also for the life you see tomorrow.

Use this quote before you fall asleep so you can remember to say thank you for the life you are about to receive.

Every time you fight through fear, make it the grateful thought you have in the morning.

You need to have a plan every morning to tell yourself all the great things you have in life. Before you set foot out of bed, this must be the first action you take. As soon as you open your eyes to the day ahead, you need to be grateful for the life you have been given. Once you begin to change the way you think, you will have many things to be thankful for. When you fight through fear and do something that brings you closer to your goals, make sure you are grateful for the courage.

Take a moment every morning and give thanks for finding the courage to use fear as direction and not deflection. Every time you conquer fear, it will no longer exist. You are not only stronger with every fear that passes, but you will have a grateful thought that will start your day. Don't waste it.

Use this quote every morning after you have conquered a fear that has been controlling your life.

If you think giving back is for the rich, you have made a choice never to have wealth.

I cannot express how important it is to give something back every day you walk this earth. It may be stopping a stranger in a crowded street to ask if they need a hand getting to their destination or giving up your weekend to serve a charity. Make no mistake, this will give you the ability to see your dreams with more clarity and give you a stronger passion for fighting for your vision. Giving back will be a powerful action you take on your journey. Make sure you do not miss its importance or the dreams you create will be lost underneath selfishness. I don't care what your story is today because I know for sure that you can give something. Money should never be a benchmark of your charity.

Use this quote when you see an opportunity to help someone in need and you decide you don't have the resources to contribute.

Make it your purpose to give your time to a cause that you truly believe is worth someone else's purpose.

You may have a great idea of ways you can help someone in need or a cause that is near and dear to your heart. If this is the case, start planning today to start giving as much time as you can to support this cause. If you don't have a cause that comes to mind, I believe you can find someone in your life who has a purpose that is worth your time and energy. If you believe in the work they do, you should join their cause and start giving back today. This will open greater opportunities for you to give back to the community and find your purpose for giving every day.

Use this quote when you think you have nothing in life that is worth giving your time for.

Give to someone else when you think you cannot and you will find the riches you desire.

To have the success and wealth you desire, you must find time in your day to help someone in need. Once you decide to make this decision and stop formulating reasons why you cannot, you will soon grasp the power of this act. When you tell yourself you don't have the time or the money to help someone in need, that is the life you will create. You will not have the money or the time because you have made that decision. Once you understand the power of giving back every day, the feelings you acquire will support your vision.

Once you live every day actively looking for ways you can help someone in need, you will create different paths to achieve your goals. It may seem selfish at times, but once you live this way, you will understand its power. Giving back is not a choice if you believe in my way of thinking; it is a prerequisite.

Use this quote when your attitude toward giving starts to become selfish and you decide to look away.

Always be grateful for what you have and what you desire will be what you are grateful for tomorrow.

Every day say thank you for all the great things you have in life. You may not have everything you want in life, but do not skip this step. They may be sizable or they may be slight, but treasure the value of life. It could be the love you have for family or a vacation you are about to take. Not everything in your life is atrocious, so make sure you recognize and acknowledge the things that bring you joy. Be grateful for what you have today and the world will create more things you will be thankful for tomorrow.

When you do this daily, the life you envision will start to manifest in front of your eyes. Incorporate this act in your morning routine and throughout your day. Before you leave your house, you need to do this simple but essential task. Not only will it provide perspective, but it will also train your mind to see that your life isn't a disaster. When this happens, you need to be grateful for this gift. Be grateful for what you have today and you will be given things throughout your day that will help you accomplish your goals of tomorrow.

Use this quote as soon as you open your eyes and before you fall asleep to train your mind never to forget this step in your daily routine.

Dream Big and Believe

When you are unsure of the direction you need to take, believe in the dream and the path will present itself.

We can get so caught up in how our dreams will come to life that we spend too much time trying to figure out what the path looks like. You may have the perfect idea in your mind, but when you analyze the possible routes, you start to question if you're wasting your time. If you cannot see any possible paths that will lead to your dreams, no way will be constructed. Every time you think the road is a dead end, your dream loses velocity. You need to refocus your mind on the end result of your vision and the feeling it will create. Have faith that a path will find you. It may be hard to do, but you must stop worrying about how your dream will manifest and continue to focus on your goals with an unwavering belief that the path will be constructed.

Use this quote when every possible road you see to accomplish your dream seems to lead to a dead end.

Command your mind to be in a place where you dream.

Being in a state of positivity is extremely difficult at the beginning. Not only do you have to think differently, but you must train your mind to fight your negative thoughts every day. Whenever negativity enters your mind, you need to find a way to command yourself to think of the positive vision you are working toward. When you don't have the tools to rise from negativity, you will be forced back into a life that brings you no excitement. The negative people and thoughts will not disappear because you have a different mindset about life. They will still be present, but if you choose to see life with a positive mind, they will look different. Their effect on your life will be minimized when you maximize the power of your mind and your purpose.

Use this quote when negative thoughts enter your mind and remember you have ultimate control.

You can be or do anything in this world if you can see it clearly enough to believe it already exists.

The world you live in today is a result of the thoughts you create and the corresponding actions to those thoughts. If the world you see today doesn't bring you happiness, then you have a choice to change your thoughts to produce different results. Actions may speak louder than words, but your thoughts will create your future. Once you have clearly decided how you want your future to look, you need to picture it daily. Not a hopeful feeling but a belief that it already exists.

If you dedicate yourself to thinking and acting as if the life you envision is already yours, every action you take will bring you closer to its reality. Everything that surrounds you was created by a thought that produced action. If you truly believe the vision of your future exists, your thoughts will produce actions louder than your circumstances.

Use this quote when you have a hard time believing in your vision so you can focus on acting like you are living your dream.

The sun will shine every day when you decide to believe in the sun.

Every morning, when we open our eyes to a new day, checking the weather is as normal as brushing our teeth. We may reach for our phones or swipe the curtain in anticipation of what the day will bring. If the sun is not shining, we tend to let it affect our mood and how we attack our day. The same is true for our dreams and vision for the future.

As soon as a cloud of doubt slowly starts to shift and cover our vision, we tend to lie back down and let our negativity take over. When you believe your dreams still exist despite the clouds, the skies will open with possibility. Even on the gloomiest of days, we must believe the sun is still shining behind the clouds. The sun will never leave you and will continue to shine no matter how strong the storm blows. Believe in your dreams every day and your sun will shine despite the weather.

Use this quote on days when the weather brings you down and remember your vision still exists.

Never underestimate the power of persistence when your path is surrounded by passion.

Once you realize what your passions are in life, you cannot give up fighting every day to create the place where you dream. I came up with this quote many years ago when I thought it would be nice to write for a living.

It has always resonated with me, but I have never really pursued it the way I originally intended. Deep down, I didn't believe it was possible. I knew a long time ago what I wanted in life but decided in my mind after a couple of failed attempts that it was impossible.

If you have a passion, you cannot stop working and trying anything and everything to make it come alive. If you choose to believe your passion can become your career, the path will be shown.

You must take steps every day to make this possible and know that the path is being created through your belief. Don't worry about how the path will be created or which road you must take right now. Through persistence and faith, your passion will guide you to the right path.

Use this quote when you are looking to turn your passion into a career but start to lose faith.

The perfect world can exist when you have the courage to create a thought through imagination.

Everyone in this world has an idea of what the perfect life would look like. They imagine winning the lottery and sitting on the beach with a cold beer and a warm smile, but in a moment, they awaken to their reality. Having a dream is a great start, but you must believe it's possible.

If you don't believe winning the lottery will ever happen, stop spending your time imagining how great that life would be. Start to imagine how great life would be if you had everything the lottery would provide. Focus on the beach—not the ticket.

The ticket you dream of cashing in cannot be purchased. It can, however, be found when you realize it has been in your possession the whole time. You may have to move around some negative thoughts, but it's real. It can be found when you are willing to believe it exists.

If you believe you can feel the sand between your toes, your ticket will start to form the numbers needed to hit the jackpot. When you find the courage to taste the hops from your freshly poured beer before it was ever brewed, you will never buy another lottery ticket.

Use this quote when you think winning the lottery is your only option for success.

Faith is not something you save for Sunday; it is the fire that should ignite each and every day.

Faith is a very tricky word that people tend to shy away from or completely embrace. I am not a religious man by conventional standards, but know my faith is something I will never disregard as I change the way I think. The religion I use daily is the belief that the dreams and goals I have found are possible. Once I took away the doubt I held for so many years, I finally found peace and purpose. If this is what a religious man sees every day, I will never question a man's faith in God. Like faith in God, your faith in your future must be held with the same conviction.

I believe the Bible is the greatest selling book of all time because it communicates in detail a universal truth to all humankind. As you believe, so it shall be done unto you. Use the belief in your dreams to awaken the voice you have been afraid to alter. We all hear a voice every day that tells us the direction we need to take to become the best version of ourselves. We should choose to listen to its wisdom for more than one day a week.

Use this quote when you don't feel like using faith in your daily routine.

Take off the glasses you have been forced to wear if you cannot see the beauty that surrounds you.

Throughout our lives, we are transformed from an innocent child with the power of imagination into an adult who only sees what's in front of our eyes. You may not remember the moment this happened, but sometime in your life, you started to see life with limitations and not what was possible in your mind. The glasses you wear today were given to you in the form of fears and limitations. They only let you see a life that is unattainable and not possible because they are not the right prescription.

You may not realize you have put on these glasses, but once you dare to take them off, you will see life with a clarity that you forgot existed. When these glasses are removed, you will experience life with twenty-twenty vision.

Use this quote so you can take off the store-bought glasses that will not strengthen your vision.

The difference between hope and belief lies in how you choose to see your future. Live in a future that already exists.

This quote has lifted me from so many days of uncertainty. I cannot measure its influence. Before I hit my first keystrokes to write this book, I used the word "hope" dozens of times during a given day. Once you decide to change your thoughts into a more positive vision, you will start to question the definition of hope. I always hoped for things to be better, but my wishes were never answered. I now understand that I was using the incorrect word and the wrong state of mind.

Pay attention when you choose to use the word "hope" in relation to what you are looking to accomplish. When you hope for something in life, there is a question in your mind. You leave the possibility that other outcomes are plausible. When you start to replace the word "hope" with belief, your world will change. I no longer hope for anything; I believe, without a doubt, that I will get whatever beauty I choose to see and whatever I am expecting.

Use this quote anytime you say the word "hope."

With the power of belief, realize your dream to find the strength to open your eyes.

We all have the power to realize our dreams, but sometimes we choose to close our eyes to the opportunities that surround us. We are so focused on our daily lives that we never take a moment to dream. We race through our days with thousands of thoughts and images in our mind. These thoughts are surrounded by daily tasks and chores that suppress our dreams.

We never go after our dreams because we have closed our eyes to the possibility that they can be realized. If you don't believe in your dreams, you will never find a way for them to become a reality. Once you have found the perfect vision of your future, you must put every thought and feeling behind the belief that it is possible. When you truly believe in your dreams, your eyes will open and opportunities will no longer be repressed.

Use this quote anytime your daily tasks close your mind to an opportunity.

If you cannot express your dreams and desires to the ones you love, you must find the confidence that your dreams are possible.

Once you have decided what your dreams and goals are in life, you need to leverage the people around you. There is a network of people willing to help you accomplish your goals, but you must involve them in your plans. If you do not tell them what your goals are, they cannot find ways to help you succeed. Your confidence may just be developing, but you need to stand tall and pronounce that your belief in your goals is stronger than your insecurities.

It may be difficult to tell the ones you love about your lofty goals because you may be afraid of their response. If you feel the urge to hold back from telling them your dreams, you need to step back and reevaluate whom you surround yourself with. You need to understand that your hesitation is a result of your lack of confidence in yourself. If you don't believe your dreams are possible, you cannot express the inevitability of their conclusion.

Use this quote when you hesitate to tell the ones you love your new mindset and the dreams you now work toward.

Success is not the words we speak but the belief in the power of our words.

To be successful, you need to define success. Is your definition of success based on someone else's views or your own? We all see success differently, and it's up to you to create your own definition. Do not let others define success for you. Once you have a clear definition of success, you then have a goal. Make sure you use the right words to describe this goal and make sure your words have conviction. Words mean nothing if they have no energy behind them. I hope you can feel the passion in my words, but these words are mine. If you are looking for success, you first need to define what that means. Once you have the words, you are now ready to speak your truth.

Use this quote when you have defined success so you can understand that words mean nothing until you believe in the power they create.

When we choose to live life as others expect, we are not living our life but someone else's.

Do not let others' expectations limit your vision and your dreams. Remember that they are limited because they choose to see life as they have been taught. They do not have the knowledge or belief that life can be more than their circumstances. Experiences formulate expectations. Your experiences create the expectations that build a ceiling of what is possible. You have been taught that you can only receive a particular life because no one has shown you a life without limitations.

The ceiling was created because others have been trained to gently place their fingers against the glass and tell you it exists. You must remove your fingers from the glass and use your hand to open the door for everyone trapped inside this dirty glass. It may be a hard cycle to break, but once you understand why others' expectations are so small, you will start to build a life without ceilings and limitations.

Use this quote when you try to explain your goals to someone who cannot see any possible way they can be achieved.

Nothing in life is out of reach if you haven't reached for it.

We all have things in life that we love to do and things that can create limitless pride. There are times in our lives that restrict us from reaching for our dreams and make us retreat. It may be fear of the unknown or doubt that pushes our ideas to a place where they seem invisible. It is such a powerful feeling that we never attempt to reach. If there is something in your life that once was within your grasp, you need to recapture the time when you believed it was possible.

If you believe without a doubt in your mind that this dream is worth your resources, reexamine your purpose. If you don't have an intention to do the things you love every day, you will never reach true happiness. Reach for the dream you have been afraid to touch if you truly believe it is worth holding. Nothing is out of reach when you have the tenacity to grab the dream others think is untouchable.

Use this quote when you have a dream that others believe to be impossible and unreachable.

Never hide your face when you can clearly see the path. Surround your path with the faces that believe the path is real.

You may be hesitant to tell anyone about your new way of thinking. You may be afraid that they will laugh at your newly established goals. Once you are clear about the goals and dreams you have for your future, your voice must be resounding. Be careful who you share your vision with, but never hide your intentions from those who will embrace and support your new passion for life. If you don't tell anyone about your goals, you may never find the right direction.

Your supporters will become crucial to paving the path that will guide you to the life you always wanted to walk. They might have ideas that can clear the path you now travel every day. Don't let skeptics and laughter block your path. Surround your path with the ones who will help you achieve your goals.

Use this quote when you are afraid to tell a loved one about your dreams and goals.

Leaders are not born into greatness but created through a belief and a passion that they can lead.

We are all born with innocence and gifts that can make us great. No one is born a leader. We are given different upbringings and people who guide us in life. Leaders are created because they believe they have been born to lead. They don't use excuses or circumstances to explain failure; they use failure to fuel success.

They understand that true belief will bring people and resources to accomplish any dream or goal they can imagine. They know that, with time and trust in their goals, they can inspire others to join their journey. Their conviction is so firm that others have no choice but to follow. Passion is infectious, and belief is contagious. With confidence and conviction, you can become a leader who can inspire, but you must believe that you can lead.

Use this quote when you think you were born to follow.

Always be aware of your surroundings as you change the way you think and feel.

Every day you choose to change the way you think is an important day. It is important because once you make the decision, you will start to hear the whispering voice you once ignored. It will be so quiet you will squint your eyes to listen.

You may have heard a version of this voice before, but make no mistake, this voice will guide your new life. Don't doubt its importance and don't underestimate its significance if you are truly in tune with your unique vision. Be aware of your surroundings because the answers you seek already exist.

Every day you need to be fully conscious of what you see and hear because when you believe in your dreams, clues will be presented. These clues may be obvious or they may be subtle. It is entirely up to you how these pieces will fit your puzzle. Make sure your mind is ready to receive direction from this whispering voice so you can stand tall and listen intently.

Use this quote when your belief in your dream is strong and you search for answers and direction.

Success isn't measured in dollars; it's who you become that will define success.

Some of the most successful individuals in the world are not happy. We call them successful because of their bankroll. They may be successful on paper, but they are not fulfilled. They may have the possessions that we lust for, but the rest of their life is empty. They have a team of people who follow their every move and drop everything when they make a request. If this is all you want in life, consider your dream a success. For me, success looks different.

The million-dollar house I see is full of the family and friends that have joined me on my journey. I have the money I need to provide for my family, but I also have the time to enjoy their company. If building an enterprise is all you need to be a success, follow that dream. Just make sure you have a clear vision of who you want to become and not what others see as success.

Use this quote anytime you feel your direction is not giving you everything you need to succeed.

Darkness becomes distant when your eyes race to open and experience life with an angelic look of simplicity and unwavering belief.

We can all see a form of darkness in our lives. It may be why you decided to read this book. Darkness and light are opposites because of what they represent. You may see the light as opportunity and darkness as misfortune. The one you choose to see throughout your day is your decision.

They are both present, and they can both provide perspective. You can choose to see the darkness that surrounds your life or you can decide to find opportunities you may not have been willing to see. You need to stop walking in darkness and run toward the positive thoughts you have forgotten that exist in your mind. The task is simple, but the road will be dark if you are not willing to believe that your dream is possible. Unwavering belief is such a hard feeling to obtain, but when you embrace its light, the darkness will become distant. Give yourself the chance to believe you can be great.

Use this quote when your spirit is broken and your belief is wavering.

If your future is a picture you cannot quite see, you must ask yourself if you are looking in the right direction.

Finding the perfect picture can be a tricky part of your journey because most of us are afraid to ask for exactly what we want in life. We start by asking for things we think are attainable. When you find the audacity to ask for something impossible, you will have a hard time believing it will ever happen at first. This is when you need to look in a different direction.

The doubt you feel is understandable, but you need to investigate the future and feel the joy this impossible dream would create. If you can't quite see it today, then you need to fight harder. Strengthen your mind so the direction you seek will be clear in your mind. See yourself living your dreams and you will soon have a perfectly framed picture of what already exists.

Use this quote when you think your dream is too big and you start to look toward a life that someone else believes is attainable for you.

Never question yourself when you think you are not enough; ask yourself if you want something better and accept its arrival.

If you want something better in life, you need to dream bigger. If you think you are not enough today, this is the perfect moment to ask yourself what would make you happy. Once you question why you have settled for the life you live, you will have answers as to why you think you are not enough. You can accomplish any dream you can conceive. You should never question yourself until you are ready to accept your dream as the key to your happiness.

Use this quote when you question the potential your biggest dream can have on your happiness and accept that it exists.

Unwavering belief may be the most difficult feeling to attain, but when you grasp its power, the gates will open automatically.

I first heard these words as I was searching for inspiration and scouring YouTube for motivational speeches that could give me direction. I listened to many great speakers over my years and have been given some great advice. When the words "unwavering belief" softly entered my mind, I immediately wrote them down on my whiteboard next to "milk" and "bread." I gained great perspective when I realized what it represented. Unwavering belief is tough to attain and even more challenging to keep. It will be challenged every day by those who refuse to believe their dreams are possible. Once this feeling dominates your mind, the gates will open to display a life that has multiple entrances.

Use this quote when you have doubts about your new way of thinking.

One focused thought is a hundred times more powerful than ten ideas without the belief they are possible.

You need to stay focused on your goals and the life you want to create. Once you lose focus, you will lose any progress you have made. Every day you need to spend a significant amount of time imagining the life you want to create. You need to force your mind to believe your unbelievable dreams are possible. Train your mind to start focusing on your goals when you start to sway into normality.

We all have dreams of the perfect job or new car, but deep down we don't really believe we could have these luxuries. We imagine a better life but never think it could happen. We focus on the fact we will never receive these gifts, and that thought gains power. If it's a new car you want, choose to focus on putting yourself behind the wheel. You may not know how you will get this car, but when you concentrate on driving, the power will be magnetic.

Use this quote when your mind starts to wander and your focus is spread too thin.

Do not reach for the fruit you can touch; climb the tree you choose to see.

Sometimes in life, we are presented with the low-hanging fruit. We do not have to walk a long path or look beyond our reach. It dangles with ease right in front of our eyes. It may be easy to obtain, but do we really know if it has the nutrients needed to grow and flourish? Once you believe your dream is possible, this seedling will start to show more robust branches. It will grow and mature with every positive thought you place at its root.

In a short time, you will observe a perfectly positioned fruit gently dangling from the highest branches waiting for your arrival. You will have to climb to the top to enjoy this colorful and fruitful display, but when you decide to climb one branch at a time, the taste will be delectable.

Use this quote when your only vision for the future contains opportunities that are easily obtained.

If you think your dream is too big to accomplish, then it is the perfect size.

Never be afraid to dream big when the world seems small. We tend to give our attention to things that are attainable while our biggest dreams sit on an imaginary wish list. These dreams sit in the back of our mind for decades until we are too cold to feel the warmth they could provide. If you think your dream is too big, it is only because you don't have the belief that it is possible. What if your dream could come true and you could live the life you always imagined? If you have a dream that has been resting in emptiness, you need to give it the power to stand. Your dream must be realistic, but when you believe it's possible, no dream is too big. Small-minded individuals will always put a size on dreams. If you don't dream of paradise, be prepared to lie down and cross your arms in cessation.

Use this quote whenever you have a dream you think is too big to accomplish.

When you dream big and think positive thoughts, a simple vision can become reality and your future is only the fantasy you choose to believe.

Never limit yourself to a vision that you think is attainable. Imagine an improbable life and imagine it every day with the belief that it is possible. We tend to dream of situations and outcomes that we believe are attainable because we can see scenarios where they come to life. We continue to think this way because we were never given a different perspective on all that life can provide. Imagine if the biggest dream you could conceive was possible.

The difference between fantasy and reality is how you choose to see outcomes. When you choose fantasy, you leave too much room for different scenarios to transpire. You are not 100 percent sure it will happen. When you believe in only one outcome, only one outcome can be your reality. The ideas of success that have been force-fed to us our entire lives are not finite. They are just the reality that we choose to believe. Once you start to think beyond what others believe is possible and start to tap into your positive thoughts, your fantasies will become achievable. Dream bigger than the reality you see today and you will soon become a part of your fantasy.

Use this quote when your dreams and goals start to become products of your peers.

Final Quote

The final quote in this book was not written by my hand because I have found a voice that needs a purpose. A voice that once had the passion for walking down a crowded street and finding focused inspiration only he could create. In the confusion that now surrounds his life, this voice has been misplaced.

This voice now lies in a darkness that can only be seen through dozens of poems that have no purpose but to fuel unhappiness. Depression and doubt have displaced his voice and pushed him into a world of seclusion and pessimism. It has created a man who is unable to see the power of belief and what is possible. I asked my brother to write the last quote in this book because I believe the pen he writes with today needs to be replaced. He may write every day to release emotions he cannot control, but the pen he chooses to grasp has a darkness that continues to hold his mind hostage.

I believe he has the ink to inspire, but he needs to grip a different pen. Once he understands that one positive thought has the power to release the negativity he has been holding in his hand, he will be free. I hope this quote will be a positive thought that will start a transformation I know is possible.

When I see him struggling every day to find his purpose, it propels me back to the moment I opened my eyes to a new way of thinking. There was a time not too long ago when I felt the same depression and doubt he faces today. I can see my past reflection in his eyes and can distinctly hear a voice that once told me my dreams were impossible.

His passionless voice reminds me of why I fight every day to live in a place where I dream. I have made a promise to myself that this voice will never be a part of my future, and I promise my brother the same. He may be a few steps behind, but I believe the words he has found within this quote will start a belief that he can capture a dream without confusion. Once he is clear as to what it is he wants from life, I promise I will be right beside him as he takes every monumental step.

Although I was not present when he started to lose his innocence, I will make it my purpose to stand tall as he rises from the life he thinks has already been written. Soon we will write a story that will be seen through the words we create together—a script soon to be written with a pen we find as brothers.

I am so proud of my brother for finding the words to start his journey toward positivity. I asked him to write the final quote because I know that he is one positive thought away from freedom. With these words, I believe he will become a man who is not afraid to be weak but proud to be strong.

To predict the passion of perception and design the destiny desired, you must deteriorate the attachment of safety. Fall within the flood of fantasy between the fear.
—Dylan Edwards

Written with moonlit lead, these words surrendered my soul. Teetering on the ledge of comfort, I let my passion push me further into uncertainty. Every emotion became transparent. For too long I lived without a vision and with nothing to reach for or pursue. Allowing my mind to impair my passion, I watched the lights dim as my spirit struggled to survive. Lost in the world I created, my thoughts and fears suppressed the destiny I was unable to perceive. Confused continuously and caught in the chaos, I fought the termites attacking my soul. With every piece that was taken, I struggled to reach for the remains. I analyzed every thought scratching the surface as my fear suddenly appeared.

This fear wasn't bold nor frantic but hidden within my spirit. Beneath the blanket covered in comfort, I held on for safety. Cautious of the outcomes and negative thoughts, I avoided the positive possibilities and was subconsciously persuaded to settle.

Held captive by my circumstances, I am attempting to attack the time I have left to design my desires with every ounce of optimism wrapped within these words. Guiding my mind to penetrate past the perception of negativity and negligence, these words relinquished my soul from the mist and I found my forever flood.

I faced two options: an ocean filled with fantasies or a puddle of poor possibilities. Pushed to the only path, I dove inside the waves. With every word I speak, I search to see success in spiritual bliss before any occurring battle I face. My heart has fallen in harm to so many unseen situations that I never chanced.

Impatiently I stood by and watched as I tried to understand what could have been. With time I have detached my blanket of safety and uncovered the constant comfort that has been holding my mind hostage.

My heart decided to become perpetual in my passion when I chose to see what my soul craves. Listen to the love seeping from your heart and never wait. Allow yourself to see the potential you hold instead of wishing for what could unfold. Your soul is yours, and no one can take away the desires you have.

Dedicated to my brother Topher. The only one who showed me what I could be if I only opened my mind.

Closing Thoughts

I have not written this book to tell anyone how to live his or her life. This book was written because I believe that if you want the life you have always imagined, then it's possible. Why should you settle for a life that doesn't bring you a passion for rising every day?

A life that includes the negative thoughts you have been holding in your mind.

Maybe you have everything you want in life, and perhaps everything in life is exactly how you envisioned it would be. If this is true, I would like to say congratulations.

This book was written for the person who is one positive thought away from getting the life they always imagined was possible.

You may not understand the power of belief today, but I hope my words will make a difference in how you see the impact your positive thoughts can have on tomorrow. There is more to life than a nine-to-five job if a nine-to-five schedule isn't what you see. I would never say that my words can get you the experience you have always desired, but I can say that I believe in the words I have written.

I truly believe I will get everything I want in life because I see its beauty in my mind every single day. Nothing in this life is impossible if you believe in the gift you have been given. Take control of your mind and allow yourself to dream bigger.

I am so close to getting everything I want in life, and this book was my first thought-provoking action. I'm ready to embrace a new existence, and I can't wait to write my next chapter so I can tell all my readers that the unreachable is possible.

One of the most important things I have learned on my journey is the power of saying thank you.

I want to say thank you to everyone who read this book and joined my journey toward the life I have now achieved. You are only a thought away from capturing everything you have always imagined was possible.

Words can't express the gratitude I feel to those who have become part of my migration and helped me accomplish my goal of becoming an influential and successful writer.

I have so many more words and thoughts that I'm ready to release and I'm so grateful that I have the courage to dream bigger.

I believe you are about to start a journey that is worth every dream you have been afraid to free. Understand you have the power to create the life you see in your dreams if you choose to believe it's possible. Just believe!

***

Pick up Volume II of the *101 Quotes Series* now and see how my voice has changed in the five years following this book.

Grab Volume II*: 101 Quotes That Will Expand Your Mind* right now at Amazon or visit *topherpike.com* for more info.

A Letter to Sophia

My journey will not be complete if I don't create a way to give my daughter everything she desires in life. I will do whatever it takes to provide Sophia with every tool she needs to dream big.

Dear Sophia,

I believe this book will be the start of your belief that your dreams are possible. My greatest goal in life is to provide for our family and guide you to a life you deserve. I will not let you waste the precious time you have. I promise that you will be fully equipped to take on a world that will try to crush your hopes and dreams with fear and normality. I will not only teach you the most important skills to succeed in life, but I will also show you step-by-step how to apply these skills. Together we will formulate a plan that will take you from an innocent child to a woman who is confident enough to fight for your passion.

The joy I feel today has pushed me to be a better man, and I will not waste my gift by letting the ink fade. I will force my mind and my thoughts to create a life that is worth the love of my family.

I will never stop pushing every day because of fear. I will fight every day, knowing that my fear is not real and my belief in possibility is more powerful than the script I was given. I will push every day with knowledge of power I cannot touch but a gift I will teach. One positive thought will have absolute power over depression and doubt.

I will show you that to change your world you must change the perception of the world that has been presented. Present yourself to the world with a vision surrounded with purpose and the world will offer a new path toward your passion. I am so grateful that I have the gift to see life as a story that has not been written.

I will not let you pick up the book that has been perfectly placed on a beautifully built bookcase in the front of a store purposely marketed to the masses. I will teach you about a book that has never been written by an author of your choosing. This book may be in the deepest part of the bookstore and covered in the dust of a thousand beautiful minds, but this book will ignite a passion with the power of one positive thought. It can only be written by the one who turns the empty pages and believes in the words only he or she can create.

Your story is unwritten until you decide to put pen to paper. I will give you a pen every day to help you find the words to write your own story. A story worth your heart and your soul. Believe me when I tell you that you are the creator of your own life, and never let anyone tell you it can't be done. I have written you these words for one reason. When they try to feed you the book of mediocrity, you will be perfectly prepared to answer with one statement.

I will never choose to take the book that has been presented to me by the masses who pretend to understand my dreams and desires. I will choose to find the empty book and put my pen to paper.
—*Sophia Pike*

I will give you every opportunity you need to write your story with a passion only you can find. I will soon need your help to pass the pen to my next vision, whose innocence can only be found in the picture I have seen through the love of family. The heartbeat may be faint, but with the faith we find as a family, you will soon become the teacher.

Author Notes

Words mean nothing without action, so I decided to add this section to help you find the direction to realize your dream. Writing this section was not my intention when I started to write this book. I only wanted to get my thoughts on paper and share my ideas with others looking for a different path. I realized after multiple readings of my book that something was missing. I could not leave my thoughts without action. I hope this book will be the start of your journey, but if you are truly ready for change you must act now. Grab the biggest pen you can find and start writing a new ending to the story of your life. Your future is now in your hands.

The first challenge I will give you is finding your purpose. This will be your most difficult challenge. Your purpose in life lies somewhere between your dreams and your passions. Think about your five greatest passions in life and write them down on paper with purpose.

My second challenge is attacking your fears. Your fears will lose power once you are strong enough to write them down confidently then forcefully cross them off this list. Write down your top five fears and make it your mission to cross them off as soon as possible.

The third challenge will be extremely important as you fight your negative thoughts. Write down five things in life that make you smile. Use these feelings to replace any negative thought that enters your mind and remember that your happiness is within your control.

The fourth challenge will help you realize all the great things you have in life. No matter what stage you are at in life I am positive that you can find five things to be grateful for today. Start your list by being grateful for what you have and finish with what you are grateful for in the future.

The fifth and final challenge is to think bigger than your circumstances. Write down five things in life that if you had them you would be completely fulfilled. Write them down with a belief that you already achieved them. Use this challenge to start creating the person you want to become.

I hope you enjoyed this book and if you want a chance to get a free signed copy and other exclusive giveaways, please visit www.topherpike.com and drop your email. I promise only good stuff!

If you really want to show me some love, please visit my Patreon page at www.patreon.com/topherpike. For the cost of a cup of coffee, you can get instant access to all my work and get an insider look at unreleased manuscripts, behind the scenes access, bonus quotes, short stories, exclusive Patreon content and much more. Little princesses have expensive tastes!

If you were nice enough to buy this book and get to the end, I hope you might also be kind enough to leave me an Amazon review. Reviews are an essential part of my success as a writer, and your support is much appreciated. Just a couple of quick lines would mean a lot.

Before I sign off, I just wanted to drop a few lines to say thanks. Although we may not know each other personally, I want you to know that it really means a lot to me that you support my work. To inspire others is the reason why I write, and without your continued support, I cannot reach my full potential as a writer, husband, father, and a human being.

I'm still a long way away from my goal of 500,000 copies sold, but every word written, and every book sold gets me one step closer. Thanks again for the support and see you in the next one! P.S. Don't forget to pick up my book *101 Quotes That Will Expand Your Mind* right now on Amazon.

I wish you passion, love, and peace!

Stay inspired,

Topher Pike

Up Next

101 Quotes: Volume I – Full List

1. Attack your day with purpose or your purpose will be serving someone else's dreams and desires.

2. Don't wait for a storm to change your life; create the storm that will change your life.

3. Decide what you want in life and tell the world it's yours.

4. Tonight I will dream of a better tomorrow, but today I will awake with a vision more ambitious than yesterday.

5. If you don't know who you want to become or the life you want to live, you need to figure that out today or tomorrow will be the same as yesterday.

6. Since everything in this world is connected, be sure not to live life in a bubble of your own creation.

7. Never try to change a world you don't understand. Change yourself and your world will change with you.

8. The light that shines within doesn't have to stay within.

9. If the story of your life is in black and white, change the frequency and experience life in color.

10. Don't invent a new mousetrap; create a new mouse.

11. Change your daily habits to give your mind the freedom to create.

12. Growing isn't just about the end result; it starts with small steps and daily progress. Make progress every day and your direction will become clearer.

13. Action is not a physical motion but the response to your thoughts.

14. If you look in the mirror and see failure, look again.

15. A thousand wishes unasked are worth nothing, but one dream surrounded with passion and purpose is powerful beyond belief.

16. Don't cast judgment until you are willing to judge yourself.

17. The eyes of a leader can be seen in all those who decide to listen and believe their goals are attainable.

18. Don't reach out to me if you want to talk about the disappointment of yesterday. Only wake me if you are willing to attack today and I will be by your side.

19. Every morning, when you open your eyes and embrace your passion, encourage yourself never to fall asleep again.

20. If you think that life is not worth living, create a new life.

21. Darkness is not the absence of light; it's the absence of a purpose.

22. Strengthen your body so your mind has a place to live when you attack your day.

23. Raise the standards of how you live today to free the person you know you can become tomorrow.

24. Do what makes you happy or do nothing.

25. Happiness is easy to obtain when you decide what happy is.

26. If someone could give you everything you wanted in life by giving you one simple formula, would you walk away or walk with purpose?

27. Always be willing to embrace the moment when the power of belief overtakes your fear of failure.

28. Fear is not real when you decide it is only in your mind.

29. If a person's mind is not free of fear, can a person see clearly enough to be a witness to his or her own decisions?

30. Your wildest dreams are only a thought away once you unlock the mind that holds your doubt.

31. If you feel fear on your journey, you are on the right path.

32. One of the greatest gifts in life is knowing that your gift should never live in silence.

33. For anyone to see their future, they must be willing to put the past behind them while understanding the power and opportunity that is created from failure.

34. Never be afraid to reach for the stars, but don't forget to hold on to your vision as you choose to rise above others' expectations.

35. Your greatest defeat is your greatest opportunity to understand that defeat is powerful.

36. We all have twenty-four hours in a day, so never use time as an excuse for failure. Failure is not using the time we are given.

37. Do not look for success through an open door. Open the door where your deepest fear lies and you will find everything you need.

38. Don't hide from fear; do one thing every day that will drive your fear into hiding.

39. To change your world, you need to unleash the caged voice you have been afraid to free.

40. When you have the perfect vision of your future, hold it in your thoughts like it is the last breath you will ever take.

41. You hold the key to unlock any dream you can conceive when you understand the power you possess in your subconscious mind.

42. When the clouds pretend to block out the sun, remember that the sun is still shining.

43. If you don't believe in the power of positive thinking, you are absolutely right.

44. The world can cast a shadow over any person who is not willing to embrace opportunity.

45. When you let your dreams crawl underneath depression, you will never find the peace you desire.

46. Demand your mind to be in a good state when you feel the hand of doubt crawling down your spine.

47. Darkness surrounds your life, and so does happiness—you choose.

48. When you get angry about a bad situation, it eliminates your ability to overcome its negativity.

49. The greatest gift I have ever received is the knowledge that my wishes are heard every day by a power I can't understand.

50. The future can sometimes be seen before we are willing to accept its inevitability.

51. When you open a book, expect to see words. When you open your mind and free your thoughts, expect to see a world that you deserve.

52. When someone tells you it can't be done, remind them it is already here.

53. There is beauty in every moment once you open your mind and experience the power of clarity.

54. A good head on your shoulders is great for photographs, but a positive mind is perfectly positioned to create a bigger and brighter picture.

55. Control your thoughts; control your emotions; control your future.

56. To be successful, you must surround yourself with a successful vision. Only then should you surround yourself with success.

57. When you decide to take control of your mind, you will take control of your future.

58. Embrace the warmth of one positive thought to quickly see a light with the power and potential to be illuminated by one simple smile.

59. Happiness is the key to open a door you must walk through to obtain your hopes and dreams.

60. When the grass looks greener, and the sky seems smaller, your eyes are becoming a part of your journey.

61. Never let anyone diminish your dreams when they can't understand the power you possess.

62. Each decision we make will guide us down a gravel road surrounded by fear or a path perfectly paved with our desires.

63. Breaking through bad days is a skill, and if you don't learn to master it, you will be forever broken.

64. The future is a question only one person can answer and create.

65. When you give something back every day, the universe will understand your dreams and desires.

66. Tell the ones you love that you are grateful for their support and you will discover a gift that will fuel success.

67. Use love and gratefulness every day to get rid of pain and fear.

68. Saying thank you should never be reactive but always a proactive thought and action.

69. Start your day by saying thank you for the life you have been given and you will be given a gift that you will soon believe is possible.

70. Every time you fight through fear, make it the grateful thought you have in the morning.

71. If you think giving back is for the rich, you have made a choice never to have wealth.

72. Make it your purpose to give your time to a cause that you truly believe is worth someone else's purpose.

73. Give to someone else when you think you cannot and you will find the riches you desire.

74. Always be grateful for what you have and what you desire will be what you are grateful for tomorrow.

75. When you are unsure of the direction you need to take, believe in the dream and the path will present itself.

76. Command your mind to be in a place where you dream.

77. You can be or do anything in this world if you can see it clearly enough to believe it already exists.

78. The sun will shine every day when you decide to believe in the sun.

79. Never underestimate the power of persistence when your path is surrounded by passion.

80. The perfect world can exist when you have the courage to create a thought through imagination.

81. Faith is not something you save for Sunday; it is the fire that should ignite each and every day.

82. Take off the glasses you have been forced to wear if you cannot see the beauty that surrounds you.

83. The difference between hope and belief lies in how you choose to see your future. Live in a future that already exists.

84. With the power of belief, realize your dream to find the strength to open your eyes.

85. If you cannot express your dreams and desires to the ones you love, you must find the confidence that your dreams are possible.

86. Success is not the words we speak but the belief in the power of our words.

87. When we choose to live life as others expect, we are not living our life but someone else's.

88. Nothing in life is out of reach if you haven't reached for it.

89. Never hide your face when you can clearly see the path. Surround your path with the faces that believe the path is real.

90. Leaders are not born into greatness but created through a belief and a passion that they can lead.

91. Always be aware of your surroundings as you change the way you think and feel.

92. Success isn't measured in dollars; it's who you become that will define success.

93. Darkness becomes distant when your eyes race to open and experience life with an angelic look of simplicity and unwavering belief.

94. If your future is a picture you cannot quite see, you must ask yourself if you are looking in the right direction.

95. Never question yourself when you think you are not enough; ask yourself if you want something better and accept its arrival.

96. Unwavering belief may be the most difficult feeling to attain, but when you grasp its power, the gates will open automatically.

97. One focused thought is a hundred times more powerful than ten ideas without the belief they are possible.

98. Do not reach for the fruit you can touch; climb the tree you choose to see.

99. If you think your dream is too big to accomplish, then it is the perfect size.

100. When you dream big and think positive thoughts, a simple vision can become reality and your future is only the fantasy you choose to believe.

101. To predict the passion of perception and design the destiny desired, you must deteriorate the attachment of safety. Fall within the flood of fantasy between the fear.

Made in United States
Troutdale, OR
12/06/2024

26033927R00084